WOMEN OVE.
30
ARE BETTER BECAUSE

Written By:
Herbert Kavet

Illustrated By:
Martin Riskin

Manufactured in the United States of America

30 29 28 27 26 25 24 23 22 21 20 19 18 17 16 15 14 13 12 11 10 9 8 7 6 5 4 3 2 1

Ivory Tower Publishing Co., Inc.
125 Walnut St., Watertown, MA 02172
Telephone #: (617) 923-1111   Fax #: (617) 923-8839

WOMEN OVER **30** ARE BETTER BECAUSE...

They get lots more respect from the banking community.

WOMEN OVER **30** ARE BETTER BECAUSE...

They check to see if their blind dates have cars.

WOMEN OVER 30 ARE BETTER BECAUSE...

People start to admire their mind as much as their body.

They prefer sex to be enchanting rather than athletic.

WOMEN OVER **30** ARE BETTER BECAUSE...

They finally recognize the value of control top pantyhose.

WOMEN OVER **30** ARE BETTER BECAUSE...

Their personality doesn't change when a man is around.

WOMEN OVER **30** ARE BETTER BECAUSE...

They know how to keep a secret.

WOMEN OVER 30 ARE BETTER BECAUSE...

They know nothing is more comfortable than an old running shoe.

WOMEN OVER **30** ARE BETTER BECAUSE...

*They are resigned to the fact that they will **never** use their college education to earn a living.*

WOMEN OVER **30** ARE BETTER BECAUSE...

They can handle it when all their friends get engaged.

WOMEN OVER **30** ARE BETTER BECAUSE...

*They don't mind one bit
going to a movie alone on a Saturday night.*

WOMEN OVER **30** ARE BETTER BECAUSE...

They no longer let the men in their life talk them into fishing and camping trips.

They've learned the dang___ __ being a matchmaker.

They are not easily intimidated in traffic.

WOMEN OVER **30** ARE BETTER BECAUSE...

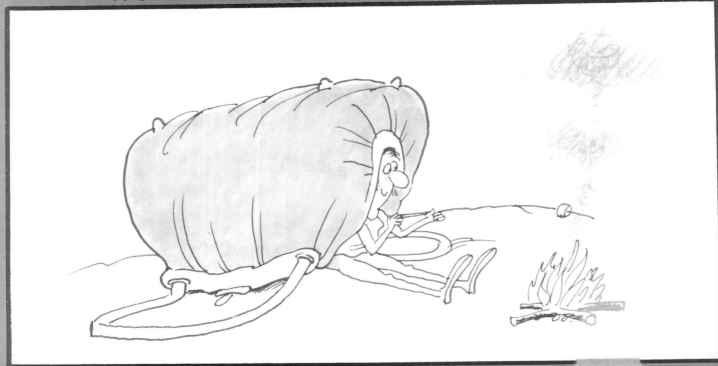

*Their handbags can sustain life for about a week
with no outside support whatsoever.*

They're finally treated with more respect at work.

WOMEN OVER **30** ARE BETTER BECAUSE...

They have a handle on the latest fashions.

WOMEN OVER **30** ARE BETTER BECAUSE...

They've learned how to dress to suit their figure.

WOMEN OVER **30** ARE BETTER BECAUSE...

They don't go on blind dates.

WOMEN OVER 30 ARE BETTER BECAUSE...

They have become bewilderingly efficient in their jobs.

WOMEN OVER **30** ARE BETTER BECAUSE...

They can't be talked into activities they don't like.

WOMEN OVER 30 ARE BETTER BECAUSE...

They've learned not to recommend hairdressers.

WOMEN OVER 30 ARE BETTER BECAUSE...

They occasionally clean their ovens.

They occasionally defrost their freezers.

WOMEN OVER 30 ARE BETTER BECAUSE...

They can afford to take some really exotic vacations.

WOMEN OVER **30** ARE BETTER BECAUSE...

They know just what it takes to make a man feel good.

They receive offers for credit cards on a regular basis.

WOMEN OVER **30** ARE BETTER BECAUSE...

They no longer have trouble getting into bars.

They've developed some decorating schemes of their own.

They don't freak out when their mother comes to stay for a few days.

They no longer run out of underwear.

WOMEN OVER 30 ARE BETTER BECAUSE...

They're not embarrassed to use a little ingenuity in the bedroom.

WOMEN OVER **30** ARE BETTER BECAUSE...

They understand about "closing costs."

They can buy a new car without their father's advice.

WOMEN OVER 30 ARE BETTER BECAUSE...

They've learned how to say "NO" to men bugging them for dates.

WOMEN OVER 30 ARE BETTER BECAUSE...

They can afford an occasional splurge.

WOMEN OVER 30 ARE BETTER BECAUSE...

They can program the VCR for their fathers.

WOMEN OVER 30 ARE BETTER BECAUSE...

They've started to understand the male psyche a little better.

They've reached a sort of accommodation with their pets.

WOMEN OVER **30** ARE BETTER BECAUSE...

They remember the abrasive qualities of sand
before making love on a beach.

They can fit almost all their makeup into a carry-on.

WOMEN OVER 30 ARE BETTER BECAUSE...

They're not afraid to
complain about poor workmanship on their car.

They're smart enough to handle certain chores on a regular basis.

WOMEN OVER **30** ARE BETTER BECAUSE...

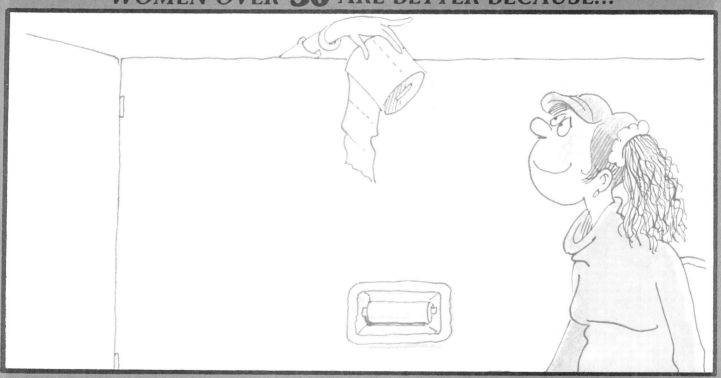

They truly know the value of a good friend.

97% of all their sex takes place in a bed.

WOMEN OVER 30 ARE BETTER BECAUSE...

They're not bashful about asking people not to smoke.

*They can eat a double hot fudge sundae
and probably not "break out."*

They are beginning to fantasize about going into business for themselves.

They realize none of the courses they took in college have the slightest value to them now.

WOMEN OVER 30 ARE BETTER BECAUSE...

They know how to organize a truly great party.

They read the reviews before they go to a show.

WOMEN OVER **30** ARE BETTER BECAUSE...

They appreciate the warmth and comfort of flannel nighties.

WOMEN OVER 30 ARE BETTER BECAUSE...

They know all the tricks for starting a car on a really cold day.

They've started to choose vacations for peace and quiet rather than action.

WOMEN OVER **30** ARE BETTER BECAUSE...

They know a few off-color stories of their own.

They don't get embarrassed introducing their friends to weird relatives.

They've stopped waiting for the baby fat to disappear.

WOMEN OVER **30** ARE BETTER BECAUSE...

*The phone and electric companies hardly ever
disconnect their service.*

*They recognize that
sex in the water is at best uncomfortable and
at worst potentially life threatening.*

WOMEN OVER 30 ARE BETTER BECAUSE...

They still look pretty good in a bathing suit.

They're intimately familiar with every diet that came along in the last 10 years.

WOMEN OVER **30** ARE BETTER BECAUSE...

They've developed total confidence in "woman's intuition."

They diet when brushing their teeth causes them to jiggle.

WOMEN OVER **30** ARE BETTER BECAUSE...

Most of their wines have corks rather than screw tops.

WOMEN OVER 30 ARE BETTER BECAUSE...

They can handle an occasional kinky request.

They are starting to acquire some matching furnishings.

WOMEN OVER 30 ARE BETTER BECAUSE...

They make plans to wash their kitchen floor.

They have an outstanding collection of bridesmaid dresses.

They know it's impossible to change people's habits.

WOMEN OVER 30 ARE BETTER BECAUSE...

They'd rather have their men successful than good-looking.

They have a few secret recipes for emergency dinners.

WOMEN OVER 30 ARE BETTER BECAUSE...

They know how to use 4 letter words at appropriate moments.

They don't blush at X-rated movies.

They finally own a car that is totally paid for.

They have learned to use restraint at big sales.

WOMEN OVER **30** ARE BETTER BECAUSE...

They can remember all their men and can definitely rate them.

WOMEN OVER **30** ARE BETTER BECAUSE...

They know their exact alcohol tolerances.

Their nightmares about exams are starting to fade.

They don't run out of toilet paper.

They're almost totally positive that horoscopes are totally bunk.

They've finally learned to ski, golf, run, or whatever rather competently.

WOMEN OVER **30** ARE BETTER BECAUSE...

They know the proper pronunciation of at least three white wines and don't let anyone bamboozle them about which goes well with what.

WOMEN OVER **30** ARE BETTER BECAUSE...

They appreciate the comfort of a few sets of sensible underwear.

They've learned that the saleswoman says,
"It's perfect for you" to everyone.

They are smart enough to hire someone to do the cleaning.

Pompous sales people no longer intimidate them.

They're resigned to the fact
that when they're dating a man over 40,
he's no longer robbing the cradle.

WOMEN OVER **30** ARE BETTER BECAUSE...

*They no longer worry very much about what
the neighbors think.*

They consider comfort when buying new shoes.

They start to make some real contributions to their field.

They no longer have to lie on their resumes.

They realize no one cares what they did in high school.

They realize the long term effects of sun on their skin.

WOMEN OVER **30** ARE BETTER BECAUSE...

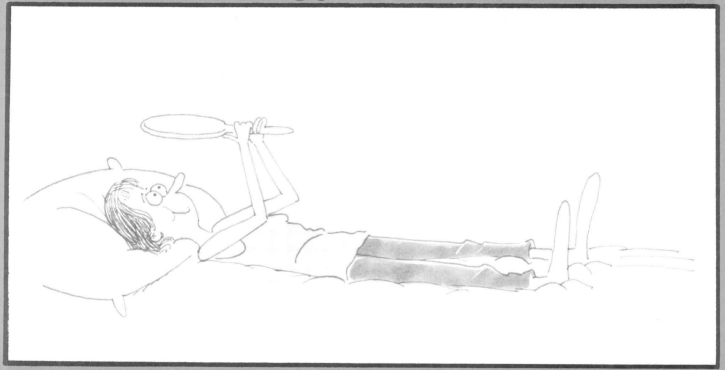

They've given up on self-improvement books, deciding they like themselves just the way they are.